AI Dictionary for Kids

Artificial Intelligence for All

By A. Onkar

Onkar Media

This AI book

belongs to

Disclaimer

Please use this as a fun and engaging way to introduce your child to the world of AI, but always consult additional resources for more detailed information.

While we've done our best to ensure that the information in this book is accurate and up-to-date, please note that it is not a complete resource and may contain omissions or errors.

We welcome any feedback or suggestions for improving future versions.

"A computer would deserve
to be called intelligent if it
could deceive a human into
believing that it was human."
- Alan Turing

In his 1950 paper (now considered an AI manifesto), Turing predicted that
around the year 2000, computers would be able to answer questions in ways
identical to those of human beings, when asked questions by a real human.

A

Activation Function
A mathematical way to process information in an A.I. program.

AdaBoost
A type of A.I. program that can make predictions about data.

Adversarial Learning
A way for A.I.programs to learn by competing against each other.

Agent
A program or machine that can make decisions on its own.

AI
A way to teach computers to do things that normally require human intelligence, like seeing, hearing, or understanding language.

Algorithm
A set of instructions that a computer can follow to solve a problem.

AlphaGo
A computer program that can play the game Go.

AlphaZero
A computer program that can teach itself to play games like chess and Go.

Anaconda
A software package that makes it easier to use certain programming languages.

ANN (Artificial Neural Network)
A type of computer program that can learn to recognize patterns in data.

Anomaly Detection
A way to find things that are different from what you would normally expect.

Apache Hadoop
A software system that helps store and manage really big amounts of data across lots of computers

Apache Kafka
A messaging system that helps send and receive big amounts of data between different software systems

Apache Spark
A software system that helps process and analyze big amounts of data really fast

API (Application Programming Interface)
A way for different software systems to talk to each other and share information

Apriori algorithm
A method for finding patterns in big amounts of data

ARIMA (Autoregressive Integrated Moving Average)
A mathematical model used for predicting future values based on past data

Artificial General Intelligence (AGI)
An artificial intelligence system that is as smart and capable as a human

Artificial Intelligence (AI)
The ability of machines to do tasks that normally require human intelligence, such as learning, reasoning, and problem-solving

Artificial Intelligence Markup Language (AIML)
A programming language used to create chatbots and other conversational AI applications

Artificial Neural Network (ANN)
A type of artificial intelligence system modeled after the structure and function of the human brain

Artificial Neural Networks (ANNs)
A collection of interconnected artificial neural networks used to process and analyze big amounts of data

Association Rule Learning
A method for finding relationships and connections between things in big amounts of data

Attention Mechanism
A component in some artificial intelligence systems that helps them focus on specific parts of an input, such as an image or sentence

Autoencoder
A type of artificial neural network that can learn how to compress and decompress data.

AutoML (Automated Machine Learning)
A system that uses artificial intelligence to automatically select and optimize machine learning algorithms for a given task

B

Backpropagation
A method for training artificial neural networks by adjusting the weights of the connections between neurons

Bagging
A technique used to improve the accuracy of machine learning models by combining multiple models trained on different subsets of the data

Bayesian Network
A type of probabilistic graphical model used to make predictions and decisions based on uncertain information

Big Data
A large amount of information that needs special software to analyze it and find useful patterns.

BigML
A company that provides software for making predictions and decisions based on big data.

Binary Classification
A way for computers to decide between two options, like "yes" or "no" or "true" or "false."

Boosting
A way to make computer models more accurate by combining many weaker models into a stronger one.

Business Intelligence (BI)
The process of using computers to help businesses make decisions based on data.

C

CART (Classification and Regression Trees)
A way to create computer models that can be used for either predicting values or classifying data.

Cartesian Genetic Programming
A way to create computer programs using a set of simple instructions that can be combined in many different ways.

Cascading
A way to process big data by breaking it down into smaller parts and processing each part separately.

CatBoost
A type of boosting algorithm that is particularly good at working with big data.

CBR (Case-Based Reasoning)
A way for computers to make decisions by comparing new situations to similar ones they have encountered before.

CEP (Complex Event Processing)
A way for computers to analyze and make decisions based on a large number of events happening at the same time.

Chain Rule
A way to find the probability of two events happening together by breaking it down into smaller parts.

Chatbot
A computer program that can have conversations with people, often used for customer service or entertainment.

Classification
A way for computers to sort data into different groups based on certain characteristics.

Cloud Computing
A way of using computers over the internet instead of using your own computer.

Clustering
A way for computers to group together similar items based on certain characteristics.

CNN (Convolutional Neural Network)
A type of artificial neural network that is often used for image recognition.

COBOL (Common Business-Oriented Language)
A programming language that is used for business applications.

Cognitive Computing
A way of programming computers to think more like humans, by understanding natural language, images, and other forms of data.

Collaboration Filtering
A way for computers to make recommendations based on the behavior of other people.

Common Sense Reasoning
A way for computers to understand everyday situations that people take for granted.

Competing Risks Model
A way for computers to predict what will happen when there are multiple possible outcomes, such as in medical research.

Computer Vision
A way for computers to "see" and understand images and videos.

Concept Learning
A way for computers to learn new concepts by looking at examples.

Convolution
A mathematical operation that is often used in image processing.

Convolutional Neural Network (CNN)
See CNN

CRISP-DM (Cross-Industry Standard Process for Data Mining)
A way of organizing the process of analyzing data.

CUDA (Compute Unified Device Architecture)
A way of using graphics processing units (GPUs) for scientific computing.

Curated Data
Data that has been carefully selected and organized for a particular purpose.

Cybernetics
The study of how machines and living things interact.

D

D3.js
A library for creating interactive and dynamic data visualizations on the web using JavaScript.

D3M (Data-Driven Discovery of Models)
A platform that automates the process of creating and deploying machine learning models.

Data Analytics
The process of examining and interpreting data to uncover useful insights and trends.

Data Augmentation
Techniques used to increase the size of a dataset by adding variations to the existing data.

Data Cleaning
The process of identifying and correcting or removing errors, inconsistencies, and inaccuracies from a dataset.

Data Engineering
The process of designing, building, and maintaining the infrastructure required to collect, store, and process large volumes of data.

Data Fusion
The process of combining data from multiple sources to create a unified view of the data.

Data Governance
The management of data policies, procedures, and standards to ensure data quality, security, and compliance.

Data Integration
The process of combining data from different sources into a single, unified view.

Data Lakes
A large, centralized repository of raw data that can be accessed and analyzed by different teams or departments within an organization.

Data Leakage
The unauthorized disclosure of sensitive or confidential data.

Data Mart
A subset of a data warehouse that is designed for a specific department or business function.

Data Mining
The process of discovering patterns, relationships, and insights from large datasets using statistical and computational methods.

Data Privacy
The protection of personal information from unauthorized access, use, or disclosure.

Data Science
The interdisciplinary field that combines statistics, mathematics, computer science, and domain expertise to extract insights from data.

Decision Forests
An ensemble learning technique that combines multiple decision trees to improve the accuracy and robustness of machine learning models.

Decision Trees
A machine learning algorithm that uses a tree-like model of decisions and their possible consequences to predict outcomes.

Deep Belief Network (DBN)
A type of artificial neural network that uses multiple layers of hidden nodes to model complex patterns in data.

Deep Learning
A subset of machine learning that uses artificial neural networks with multiple layers to learn from large amounts of data.

Deep Q-Network (DQN)
A type of artificial neural network that uses reinforcement learning to learn to play games and other tasks that require decision-making.

DeepDream
An image processing technique that uses a convolutional neural network to find and enhance patterns and features in images.

Dense Neural Network (DNN)
A type of artificial neural network with multiple layers of densely connected nodes that can learn complex patterns in data.

Density Estimation
The process of estimating the probability density function of a dataset using statistical methods.

Differential Privacy
A technique for preserving the privacy of individuals in large datasets by adding noise to the data.

Digital Twin
A digital replica of a physical object, process, or system that can be used for simulation, monitoring, and optimization.

Dimensionality Reduction
The process of reducing the number of variables or features in a dataset while preserving as much of the relevant information as possible.

Discrete Fourier Transform
A mathematical transformation used to convert time-domain signals into frequency-domain signals.

Discriminant Analysis
A statistical method used to determine which variables best separate two or more groups or classes.

Distributed Computing
The use of multiple computers to work together on a single task or problem.

Distributed Systems
A network of computers that work together to perform a common task, often sharing data and resources.

Docker
A platform for building, shipping, and running applications in containers, which are isolated software environments.

Dropout
A technique used in machine learning to prevent overfitting by randomly dropping out some nodes in a neural network during training.

Dynamic Programming
A method used to solve complex problems by breaking them down into smaller subproblems and solving them recursively.

E

Early Stopping
A technique used to prevent overfitting in machine learning models by stopping training when the model's performance on a validation set stops improving.

Echo State Network (ESN)
A type of recurrent neural network that uses a fixed, random weight matrix for the hidden layer.

Edge computing
A computing model where data processing takes place on the edge of the network, closer to the source of the data, rather than in a centralized cloud or data center.

Elastic Net
A regularization technique used in linear regression models to balance the effects of L1 and L2 regularization.

Embedding
A method used to represent words or other data objects as vectors in a high-dimensional space, often used in natural language processing.

Ensemble Learning
A machine learning technique that combines multiple models to improve performance and reduce overfitting.

Entropy
A measure of uncertainty or disorder in a system, often used in information theory and machine learning.

Ethics in AI
The study of ethical considerations surrounding the development and use of artificial intelligence systems.

Euler's method
A numerical method used to solve ordinary differential equations by approximating their solutions through a step-by-step iterative process.

Evolutionary Algorithm
A type of optimization algorithm inspired by biological evolution, often used to find optimal solutions to complex problems.

Evolutionary algorithms
A family of algorithms inspired by biological evolution that use mechanisms like mutation and selection to generate new candidate solutions to a problem.

Evolutionary Computation
A subfield of artificial intelligence that focuses on the use of evolutionary algorithms to solve complex problems.

Expectation-maximization algorithm
A statistical algorithm used to estimate the parameters of a statistical model when some of the data is missing or incomplete.

Expert System
A computer system that uses knowledge and rules to make decisions or solve problems in a specific domain, often used in fields like medicine and engineering.

Explainability
The degree to which the decisions made by an artificial intelligence system can be understood and explained by humans.

Explainable AI
An artificial intelligence system that is designed to be transparent and easily explainable to humans.

F

F-score
A measure used to evaluate the accuracy of binary classification models, taking into account both precision and recall.

Face Recognition
A computer vision technology that uses machine learning algorithms to recognize human faces in images and videos.

False positive
A false positive is a mistake made by a computer program that classifies something as being present when it is actually absent. For example, if a spam filter mistakenly categorizes an important email as spam, it is a false positive.

Feature engineering
Feature engineering is the process of selecting and transforming data features to improve the accuracy of machine learning models. It involves analyzing the data, identifying important features, and creating new ones to improve model performance.

Feature Extraction
Feature extraction is the process of selecting and transforming data features to improve the accuracy of machine learning models. It involves identifying the most relevant features and extracting them from raw data.

Federated learning
Federated learning is a type of machine learning where multiple devices or systems collaborate on a model by sharing only the necessary information, without sharing the data. It allows for privacy-preserving machine learning, where data stays on the devices it was generated on, and models are trained collaboratively.

Feedforward Neural Network

A feedforward neural network is a type of artificial neural network where information flows in only one direction, from input nodes to output nodes, without any feedback loops. They are often used for classification and regression tasks.

Fine-tuning

Fine-tuning is the process of adjusting a pre-trained machine learning model on a new dataset to improve its accuracy for a specific task. It involves training the model on the new dataset while keeping the learned weights from the pre-training phase.

Fisher's linear discriminant analysis

Fisher's linear discriminant analysis is a technique used to find a linear combination of features that best separates two or more classes of objects or events. It is often used for classification tasks.

Forward-backward algorithm

The forward-backward algorithm is a method for computing the probability of a hidden state sequence given observed data in a hidden Markov model. It involves computing both the forward and backward probabilities, and then combining them to obtain the posterior probabilities.

Frameworks: TensorFlow, PyTorch, Keras

These are software frameworks used for building and training machine learning models. They provide tools and libraries for creating and optimizing models, and abstract away many of the details of low-level programming.

Free energy principle

The free energy principle is a theory in neuroscience and machine learning that states that the brain or a machine learning model seeks to minimize the difference between its internal model of the world and the actual world it experiences. It is often used to guide the design of neural networks.

Fuzzy Logic

Fuzzy logic is a type of logic that allows for reasoning with uncertainty and imprecision. It is used in machine learning for classification and control tasks.

G

GAN (Generative Adversarial Network)
A generative adversarial network is a type of machine learning model consisting of two neural networks that compete with each other. One network generates data, and the other network tries to distinguish it from real data. The two networks are trained together, with the goal of improving the quality of the generated data.

Gaussian mixture model
A Gaussian mixture model is a type of probabilistic model that represents the probability distribution of a set of data as a sum of Gaussian distributions. It is often used for clustering and classification tasks.

Gaussian Process
A Gaussian process is a type of probabilistic model that represents the probability distribution over functions. It is often used for regression tasks, where the goal is to predict a continuous output variable.

GDPR (General Data Protection Regulation)
GDPR is a regulation in the European Union that sets guidelines for the collection, processing, and storage of personal data. It aims to protect the privacy of individuals and give them control over their data

General Adversarial Networks (GANs)
A type of neural network used for generating new data, such as images, music, or text, by pitting two neural networks against each other in a training process.

General Purpose Computing on Graphics Processing Units (GPGPU)
Using a graphics processing unit (GPU) to perform computations that would normally be done on a central processing unit (CPU), resulting in faster and more efficient processing.

Genetic Algorithm (GA)
An optimization algorithm inspired by the process of natural selection, in which a population of potential solutions to a problem evolves and improves over time.

Gini Index
A measure of statistical dispersion used to represent the inequality of a distribution, commonly used to measure the economic inequality of a population.

Google Brain
A deep learning research project at Google, focused on developing artificial intelligence through deep neural networks.

Google Cloud AI Platform
A cloud-based platform that provides tools and services for developing and deploying machine learning models.

GPT-2 (Generative Pre-trained Transformer 2)
A large-scale neural network developed by OpenAI for natural language processing tasks, such as language translation and text generation.

Gradient descent
An optimization algorithm used to find the minimum of a function, by iteratively adjusting the parameters in the direction of steepest descent.

Graph Convolutional Networks (GCN)
A type of neural network used for analyzing and processing graph data, such as social networks or molecular structures.

Graphical models
A statistical model used to represent the conditional dependencies between variables, commonly used in fields such as computer vision, natural language processing, and bioinformatics.

GUI (Graphical User Interface)
A type of user interface that allows users to interact with a computer using visual elements, such as icons, buttons, and menus.

Hidden Markov model
A statistical model used to represent the probability distribution of a sequence of observations, commonly used in speech recognition and bioinformatics.

Hierarchical Clustering
A type of clustering algorithm used to group data points into hierarchical clusters based on their similarity to each other.

Hierarchical Reinforcement Learning
A type of reinforcement learning algorithm that involves learning a hierarchy of skills or sub-tasks, each of which can be used to solve more complex tasks.

High bias
A type of error in machine learning models where the model is underfitting the training data, resulting in poor performance on both the training and test data.

Hadoop
An open-source software framework used for distributed storage and processing of large datasets, commonly used in big data analytics.

Hamiltonian Monte Carlo
A type of Monte Carlo algorithm used for sampling from complex probability distributions, commonly used in Bayesian statistics.

Hard margin
A parameter in a support vector machine (SVM) algorithm that determines the strictness of the margin separating the different classes of data points.

HBase
A NoSQL database used for storing and retrieving large amounts of data in a distributed environment, commonly used in big data analytics.

Hebbian learning
A learning rule in neural networks that states that the strength of the connection between two neurons should increase if they are both active at the same time.

Hessian Matrix
A matrix of second-order partial derivatives used to characterize the curvature of a multivariable function.

High variance
A type of error in machine learning models where the model is overfitting the training data, resulting in good performance on the training data but poor performance on the test data.

Hopfield network
A type of neural network that can be used for pattern recognition and associative memory, where the network is trained to remember specific patterns and can later recognize and retrieve them.

Hortonworks
A company that develops and supports open-source software for data management and analysis, including Apache Hadoop.

Hotspot analysis
A type of spatial analysis used to identify areas that have a high concentration of a particular feature or attribute.

Hugging Face
A company that develops natural language processing (NLP) tools and libraries, including the Transformers library used for developing and training language models.

Hyperbolic Tangent Function
A mathematical function commonly used as an activation function in neural networks, which maps input values to a range between -1 and 1.

Hyperparameter
A parameter in a machine learning model that is set by the user, rather than learned from data, and can affect the performance of the model.

I

IBM Watson
An artificial intelligence system developed by IBM that is capable of answering questions posed in natural language, and has been used in a variety of applications including healthcare and finance.

Image Captioning
A task in computer vision where a machine learning model is trained to generate a textual description of an image.

Image classification
A task in computer vision where a machine learning model is trained to classify an image into one or more predefined categories.

Image Recognition
A general term used to refer to the task of recognizing and identifying objects or patterns within an image.

Image segmentation
A task in computer vision where an image is divided into segments or regions, each of which corresponds to a different object or part of the image.

ImageNet
A large dataset of images used for training and evaluating image classification models.

Inception
A deep learning architecture developed by Google, used for image classification and other computer vision tasks.

Inception network
A neural network based on the Inception architecture.

Inception-v3
A version of the Inception architecture used for image classification tasks, which was the winner of the ImageNet Large Scale Visual Recognition Challenge in 2015.

Incremental Learning
A type of machine learning where the model is updated with new data as it becomes available, allowing the model to continuously improve its predictions.

Independent component analysis
A statistical method used to separate a multivariate signal into independent, non-Gaussian components.

Inductive Bias
The set of assumptions or biases that a machine learning algorithm makes about the data it is trained on, which can affect the performance of the algorithm.

Inference
The process of using a trained machine learning model to make predictions on new data.

Inference engine
The component of a software system that performs the inference process, by applying a set of rules or algorithms to the input data.

Information Bottleneck
A theoretical framework for understanding the tradeoff between preserving information and reducing complexity in machine learning models.

Information gain
A measure of how much information is gained by splitting a dataset into subsets based on the values of a particular attribute or feature.

Information Retrieval
The process of retrieving information from a large collection of data, often using natural language queries.

Informed Search
A type of search algorithm that uses problem-specific knowledge or heuristics to guide the search towards a solution.

Inhibitory synapse
A type of synapse in the nervous system that can reduce or inhibit the firing of an adjacent neuron.

Input layer
The layer of a neural network that receives input data and passes it on to the next layer.

Integer programming
A mathematical optimization technique where the goal is to find the best possible combination of values, subject to a set of constraints, that satisfy the given criteria and are all integers.

Intel AI

Intel AI refers to the various products and technologies developed by Intel that are related to artificial intelligence. These include processors, software, and tools for building and deploying AI applications.

International Organization for Standardization (ISO)

A non-governmental organization that develops and publishes international standards for various industries and technologies.

Internet of Things (IoT)

A network of physical devices, vehicles, and other items embedded with sensors, software, and network connectivity that allows them to connect and exchange data.

Inverse kinematics

A method used to determine the joint parameters of a robotic arm that can cause it to reach a specified position in space.

Inverse Reinforcement Learning

A type of reinforcement learning where the agent learns a reward function by observing the behavior of an expert, rather than being told what the reward function is.

Iterative deepening depth-first search

A search algorithm that gradually increases the depth of a depth-first search until a solution is found.

J

Jaccard similarity coefficient
A measure of similarity between two sets of data that takes into account the size of the intersection and the size of the union of the two sets.

Jacobi Method
An iterative algorithm used to solve a system of linear equations.

Joint probability distribution
A probability distribution that describes the likelihood of two or more random variables occurring together.

Jupyter Notebook
An open-source web application that allows users to create and share documents that contain live code, equations, visualizations, and narrative text.

K

K-means clustering
A clustering algorithm that partitions data points into k clusters, where k is a user-defined parameter.

K-nearest neighbor
A classification algorithm that assigns a label to a new data point based on the class of its k nearest neighbors in the training data.

K-Nearest Neighbors (KNN)
A classification algorithm that assigns a label to a new data point based on the class of its k nearest neighbors in the training data.

Kalman Filter
A mathematical algorithm used to estimate the state of a system from noisy measurements.

Keras
An open-source neural network library written in Python that is capable of running on top of other deep learning frameworks.

Kernel
A mathematical function that takes two inputs and returns a similarity score between them.

Kernel density estimation
A non-parametric method used to estimate the probability density function of a random variable.

Kernel Density Estimation (KDE)
A non-parametric method used to estimate the probability density function of a random variable.

Kernel Method
A method of pattern recognition that uses kernels to transform data into a higher-dimensional space where it can be more easily separated.

Kernel methods
A family of machine learning algorithms that use kernel functions to transform data into a higher-dimensional space where it can be more easily separated.

Kernel Trick
A technique used in kernel methods to implicitly transform data into a higher-dimensional space without actually computing the transformation.

Knowledge graph
A type of database that stores information about entities and their relationships in a graph format.

Knowledge representation
How information is stored in a computer so that it can be used by programs.

Kolmogorov-Smirnov Test
A way to see if a set of data comes from a particular type of distribution.

Kruskal's algorithm
A way to find the minimum spanning tree of a graph.

L

L1 regularization
A way to reduce the size of the coefficients in a model by adding a penalty term to the loss function.

Label propagation
A way to assign labels to unlabeled data points based on the labels of nearby labeled data points.

Label smoothing
A technique to improve the generalization of a model by making the output probabilities more smooth.

Language Model
A computer program that can predict the likelihood of a sequence of words.

Large margin
A way to find a decision boundary that maximizes the distance between the boundary and the nearest data points.

Lasso Regression
A type of linear regression that can be used for feature selection.

Latent semantic analysis
A way to find the underlying meaning of words and documents by analyzing their relationships.

Layer
A group of neurons in a neural network that perform a specific function.

Learning rate
A parameter that determines how fast a neural network learns.

Least Squares Regression
A type of linear regression that minimizes the sum of squared errors.

LeNet
A type of convolutional neural network designed for handwritten digit recognition.

LGBM (Light Gradient Boosting Machine)
A type of gradient boosting algorithm used for machine learning tasks.

Linear discriminant analysis
A way to find a linear combination of features that separates classes.

Linear regression
A way to model the relationship between a dependent variable and one or more independent variables.

Linearly separable
A property of data where it can be separated into two classes by a straight line or hyperplane. For example, dots on a graph that can be divided into two groups by a line.

Local Minimum

The lowest point of a particular section of a graph. It's called "local" because it only applies to that section of the graph, not the entire graph.

Locality-Sensitive Hashing (LSH)

A technique used to search for similar items in a large dataset by mapping them to hash codes, which makes the search faster.

Log Loss

A measurement of how well a machine learning model predicts probabilities between 0 and 1. A lower log loss indicates a better model.

Logistic regression

A type of machine learning algorithm used for classification problems, where the goal is to predict whether a certain input belongs to one class or another.

Long short-term memory (LSTM)

A type of neural network that can remember information for a long time, making it useful for tasks like speech recognition and language translation.

Loss function

A mathematical formula that measures how well a machine learning model predicts output values. The goal is to minimize the loss function to improve the model's accuracy.

M

Machine learning
A type of artificial intelligence that allows computers to learn and improve from experience without being explicitly programmed.

Mahalanobis Distance
A way of measuring the distance between two data points that takes into account the correlation between different features.

Markov chain
A type of mathematical model used to describe a sequence of events, where each event depends only on the previous event.

Markov decision process
A mathematical model used in reinforcement learning to find the best actions to take in a given situation.

Matplotlib
A Python library used for data visualization, particularly for creating graphs and charts.

Max pooling
A technique used in convolutional neural networks to reduce the dimensionality of the input data by selecting the maximum value in each local region.

Mean Absolute Error (MAE)
A measurement of how well a machine learning model predicts output values. It's calculated by taking the average absolute difference between the predicted and actual values.

Mean squared error
A measurement of how well a machine learning model predicts output values. It's calculated by taking the average squared difference between the predicted and actual values.

Memory network
A type of neural network that can remember information over long periods of time, making it useful for tasks like question-answering and language modeling.

Meta-Learning
A type of machine learning that focuses on how to learn, rather than what to learn. It's concerned with finding the best learning algorithm for a given task.

Microsoft Azure
A cloud computing service provided by Microsoft, which allows users to store, manage, and analyze data on remote servers.

Microsoft Cognitive Toolkit
A software toolkit used for deep learning, which is a type of machine learning that uses neural networks.

Mini-batch gradient descent
A variation of the gradient descent algorithm used to train machine learning models, where the data is split into small batches and the weights are updated after each batch.

Minimax Algorithm
A strategy game algorithm that helps find the best possible moves for a player while also taking into account the opponent's moves.

Minimum Spanning Tree
A tree structure that connects all the nodes in a graph with the minimum possible total edge weight.

Mixed reality
A type of technology that merges the real world with virtual objects or environments in a seamless way.

MobileNet
A type of neural network architecture designed for mobile and embedded devices with limited computing power.

Model
A simplified representation of a real-world system or concept used to make predictions or understand behavior.

Model Selection
The process of choosing the best model among a set of candidate models based on how well they fit the data and their ability to make accurate predictions on new data.

Multiclass Classification
A type of machine learning problem where the goal is to predict the class of an input sample from a set of multiple possible classes.

Multilayer Perceptron (MLP)
A type of neural network architecture made up of multiple layers of interconnected nodes or neurons that can learn to classify or predict patterns in data.

Multinomial Distribution
A probability distribution used to model the outcomes of a discrete random variable with multiple possible outcomes.

N

Naive Bayes
A type of probabilistic classifier that uses Bayes' theorem to predict the probability of a sample belonging to a certain class based on its features.

Natural Language Processing (NLP)
A field of study focused on enabling computers to understand, interpret, and generate human language.

Nearest Centroid Classifier
A type of machine learning algorithm that classifies samples based on their proximity to the centroid of each class.

Nearest Neighbor
A type of machine learning algorithm that classifies samples based on their similarity to the nearest training sample.

Neural Architecture Search (NAS)
A method for automatically designing neural network architectures using search algorithms.

Neural Network
A type of machine learning model inspired by the structure and function of the human brain, made up of layers of interconnected nodes or neurons that can learn to classify or predict patterns in data.

Neuron
A computational unit in a neural network that receives input from other neurons, applies an activation function, and produces output that is sent to other neurons.

Newton's Method
An iterative optimization algorithm used to find the minimum of a function by using its derivative and second derivative.

Node
An element in a graph or tree structure that represents a point or object.

Non-Maximum Suppression (NMS)
A technique used in object detection to remove overlapping bounding boxes and keep only the most confident predictions.

Non-negative matrix factorization
A matrix factorization technique used to decompose a matrix into two or more matrices with non-negative elements.

Nonlinear regression
A type of regression analysis where the relationship between the independent and dependent variables is modeled using a nonlinear function.

Normal Distribution
A probability distribution used to model continuous random variables that tend to cluster around a central value with a characteristic spread.

Normal Equation
An analytical solution for finding the parameters of a linear regression model that minimize the sum of squared errors.

Normalization
A process of scaling data to have a common range or distribution, often used to prepare data for machine learning.

NumPy
A popular Python library for numerical computing and scientific computing, often used in machine learning and data analysis.

O

Object Detection
The process of locating and classifying objects within an image or video.

Objective function
A function that is to be optimized in order to achieve a certain goal.

One-Hot Encoding
A method of representing categorical data as binary vectors where each vector has a single element set to 1 and all other elements set to 0.

Ontology
A formal representation of knowledge that specifies concepts and their relationships to one another.

OpenAI
A research organization dedicated to developing and promoting friendly artificial intelligence.

OpenCV
An open-source computer vision library used for machine learning.

OpenMP
A programming interface used for parallel programming on shared-memory systems.

Optimization
The process of finding the best solution to a problem.

Oracle
A source of truth used to evaluate the performance of a model.

Ordinal regression
A type of regression analysis used when the dependent variable is ordinal, meaning it has ordered categories.

Outlier detection
The process of identifying data points that are significantly different from other data points.

Overfitting
When a model is too complex and performs well on the training data but poorly on new, unseen data.

P

PAC Learning
A framework for studying the generalization ability of learning algorithms.

PageRank
An algorithm used by search engines to rank web pages in their search engine results.

Pairwise Ranking
A type of learning where models learn to rank items by comparing them pairwise.

Pandas
A Python library used for data manipulation and analysis.

Parity Learning
A type of learning where the model learns to classify data based on parity, or whether the number of 1's in the input is even or odd.

Particle swarm optimization
A metaheuristic optimization algorithm used for finding the optimal solution to a problem.

Particle Swarm Optimization (PSO)
A metaheuristic optimization algorithm used for finding the optimal solution to a problem.

Pattern recognition
The process of identifying patterns in data.

PCA (Principal Component Analysis)
A technique used for dimensionality reduction by identifying the most important variables in a dataset.

Perceptron
A type of neural network consisting of a single layer of neurons that can be used for classification tasks.

Performance Measure
A metric used to evaluate the performance of a model.

Permutation Importance
A method for measuring the importance of input features by permuting their values and observing the effect on the model's performance.

PGM (Probabilistic Graphical Models)
A class of models used for representing complex probability distributions using graphical models.

Pixel
The smallest unit of an image, represented by a single point of light.

Policy Gradient
A type of reinforcement learning algorithm that learns by adjusting its actions according to the feedback it receives from the environment.

Polynomial Regression
A type of regression analysis where the relationship between the independent variable and the dependent variable is modeled as an nth degree polynomial.

Pooling
A technique used in convolutional neural networks (CNNs) to downsample feature maps.

Pooling layer
A layer in a CNN that performs the pooling operation.

Porter stemmer
An algorithm used to remove the suffixes of words in natural language processing.

Positive Definite Matrix
A square matrix in which all the eigenvalues are positive.

Posterior probability
The probability of an event or hypothesis given some evidence.

Precision
The number of true positives divided by the total number of positive predictions made.

Prediction
An estimate or guess of what will happen in the future based on past observations or data.

Preprocessing
The process of preparing data for analysis by cleaning, transforming, and normalizing it.

Principal Component Analysis (PCA)
A statistical technique used to reduce the dimensionality of a dataset by finding the most important features.

Probabilistic programming
A programming paradigm that uses probabilistic models to represent and reason about uncertainty.

Probability Density Function (PDF)
A function that describes the probability distribution of a continuous random variable.

Probability Distribution
A function that describes the likelihood of observing different outcomes of a random variable.

Probability mass function
A function that describes the probability distribution of a discrete random variable.

Progressive Growing of GANs (ProGAN)
A technique for training generative adversarial networks (GANs) that involves gradually increasing the size of the generated images.

Projected Gradient Descent
A variant of gradient descent that enforces constraints on the solution space.

Prolog
A programming language used for artificial intelligence and symbolic computing.

Prototype
A preliminary version of a product or system used for testing and evaluation.

Pseudocode
A high-level description of an algorithm or program that uses
a mix of natural language and programming language
constructs.

Public Data Set
A collection of data that is freely available for public use and
analysis.

PyT
A Python library for numerical computing and machine
learning.

PyTorch
A Python library for building and training deep neural
networks.

Q

Q Network
A neural network used in reinforcement learning to estimate the expected future rewards of different actions.

Q-Learning
A model-free reinforcement learning algorithm that learns by estimating the expected future rewards of different actions.

Quadratic Loss Function
A loss function used in regression analysis that penalizes larger errors more heavily.

Qualitative Reasoning
A type of reasoning used to model complex systems using qualitative descriptions rather than precise quantitative measurements.

Quantization
The process of reducing the precision of a numerical value by rounding it to the nearest quantized value.

Quantum Computing
A type of computing that uses quantum-mechanical phenomena to perform operations on data.

Quantum Machine Learning
A field of research that explores the use of quantum computing to solve machine learning problems.

Quantum Supremacy
The theoretical ability of a quantum computer to perform
calculations that are infeasible for classical computers.

Query
A request for information from a database or search engine.
You ask a question and the system returns a set of results
that match your query.

Queue
A data structure that stores a collection of elements in a
linear order. It works like a line in real life, where the first
person to arrive is the first to be served.

Quick Propagation
A neural network training algorithm that uses gradient
descent to update the weights and biases of the network. It's
called "quick" because it adjusts the weights and biases by a
large amount instead of a small one, which can make the
training process faster.

Quick-Propagation Neural Network
A type of neural network that uses the Quick Propagation
algorithm to train its weights and biases.

R

R Programming Language
A programming language used for statistical computing and graphics. It's often used for data analysis and visualization.

R-Squared
A statistical measure that represents the proportion of the variance in the dependent variable that is explained by the independent variable(s). It's also known as the coefficient of determination.

Radial Basis Function (RBF)
A mathematical function used in machine learning that maps the input data into a higher-dimensional space. It's often used as a basis for building neural networks.

Radial Bias
A bias term in a neural network that is based on the radial distance between the input data and the center of a group of neurons.

Radial Bias Function Network
A type of neural network that uses radial basis functions and radial bias terms to transform the input data and produce output.

Random Forest
A machine learning algorithm that builds a collection of decision trees and combines their predictions to produce a more accurate result. It's often used for classification and regression tasks.

Random search
A hyperparameter optimization technique that searches the hyperparameter space randomly instead of exhaustively. It can be a more efficient way of finding good hyperparameter values.

Random Walk
A mathematical model that describes a path taken by a particle moving in a random direction at each step. It's often used in simulations and modeling of complex systems.

Ranking
The process of ordering a collection of items based on a specific criterion, such as relevance or popularity.

RANSAC Algorithm
A robust estimation algorithm used for fitting models to data that contains outliers. It works by iteratively selecting a subset of inliers and fitting a model to them.

Raspberry Pi
A small, low-cost computer that can be used for a variety of projects, such as robotics, home automation, and education. It's often used by hobbyists and students.

Rate Coding
A coding scheme used by neurons in the brain to encode information based on the rate of firing of action potentials. It's often used as a model for artificial neural networks.

Real-Time Learning
A type of machine learning where the system learns and adapts to new data in real-time. It's often used in applications that require fast and accurate decision-making.

Recency Bias
A cognitive bias where people give more weight to recent events and ignore older ones. It can affect decision-making and memory recall.

Reciprocal Rank
A measure of the quality of a ranking algorithm that takes into account the position of relevant items in the ranking.

Rectified Linear Activation Function (ReLU)
A function used in artificial neural networks that returns the input if it is positive, and zero if it is negative.

Rectified Linear Unit (ReLU)
Another name for the Rectified Linear Activation Function (ReLU).

Recurrent Neural Network (RNN)
A type of neural network that can remember information from previous inputs and use it to influence the output.

Regression
A type of machine learning problem where the goal is to predict a continuous value, such as a number or a price.

Regularization
A technique used in machine learning to prevent overfitting by adding a penalty term to the objective function.

Reinforcement Learning
A type of machine learning where an agent learns by interacting with an environment and receiving rewards or penalties for its actions.

Reinforcement Learning (RL)
Another name for Reinforcement Learning.

Relationship Extraction
A natural language processing task that involves identifying and extracting relationships between entities in text.

Relaxation Labeling
A technique used in computer vision to assign labels to objects in an image based on neighboring objects.

ReLU
An abbreviation for Rectified Linear Unit, which is a type of activation function used in neural networks.

Remote Sensing
The science of obtaining information about objects or areas from a distance, typically through the use of satellites or aircraft.

Reproducibility
The ability to reproduce the results of an experiment or study.

Residual Network (ResNet)
A type of deep neural network that uses residual connections to make it easier to train deep networks.

ResNet (Residual Neural Network)
Another name for the Residual Network (ResNet).

REST (Representational State Transfer)
An architectural style used in web services that uses HTTP requests to access and manipulate data.

RetinaNet
A type of neural network used for object detection in images.

Reverse engineering
The process of analyzing a product or system in order to understand how it works, with the goal of duplicating or improving it.

Reversible Computing
A type of computing that uses reversible operations, allowing for energy-efficient computation.

Ridge Regression
A type of linear regression that uses L2 regularization to prevent overfitting.

Robot
A machine that can perform tasks automatically, often with some degree of intelligence.

Robotic Process Automation (RPA)
The use of software robots to automate repetitive, rule-based tasks.

Robotics
The study of robots, including their design, construction, and operation.

ROC Curve
A graphical representation of the trade-off between the true positive rate and the false positive rate of a binary classifier.

Root Mean Square Error (RMSE)
A measure of the difference between predicted values and actual values, often used to evaluate regression models.

Root Mean Squared Error (RMSE)
Another name for Root Mean Square Error (RMSE).

Roundoff Error
The difference between an exact value and an approximation due to rounding.

Routing
The process of finding the best path for data or information to travel from one place to another, especially in computer networks.

Row Standardization
A technique used to transform data so that each row has the same mean and standard deviation. This can help to make it easier to compare the values in different rows.

RPA (Robotic Process Automation)
The use of software robots to automate repetitive, rules-based tasks in business processes.

Rule-Based System
A system that uses rules to make decisions or take actions based on input data.

S

SageMaker
A cloud-based service provided by Amazon Web Services (AWS) for building, training, and deploying machine learning models.

Saliency
A measure of how much a particular part of an image or visual stimulus stands out from its surroundings.

Sampling
The process of selecting a subset of data from a larger dataset for analysis.

SAS
A software suite used for statistical analysis, data management, and business intelligence.

Scaled Exponential Linear Unit (SELU)
An activation function used in neural networks that can help to prevent the vanishing gradient problem.

Scientific Computing
The use of computers and software to solve complex scientific problems or perform scientific simulations.

Scikit-Learn
A Python library used for machine learning tasks such as classification, regression, and clustering.

Search Algorithms
Algorithms used to find a specific item or set of items in a large dataset or database.

Self-Organizing Map (SOM)
A type of artificial neural network used for clustering and data visualization.

Semantic Segmentation
The process of dividing an image into regions or segments based on the meaning or content of the image.

Semi-Supervised Learning
A type of machine learning that uses both labeled and unlabeled data to train a model.

Sensitivity
A measure of how well a model is able to identify true positive cases, or cases that are truly positive.

Sequence-to-Sequence (Seq2Seq)
A type of neural network architecture used for tasks such as machine translation, speech recognition, and text summarization.

Shallow Neural Network
A type of artificial neural network that consists of only one hidden layer.

Sigmoid Activation Function
An activation function used in neural networks that maps input values to a range between 0 and 1.

Sigmoid Function
A mathematical function that maps input values to a range between 0 and 1.

Sigmoid Neuron
A type of artificial neuron used in artificial neural networks that uses a sigmoid activation function.

Sigmoid Neuron Model
A model of the way in which sigmoid neurons in a neural network are connected and work together.

Signal Processing
The analysis, modification, or manipulation of signals, such as sound or images, to extract useful information or perform a specific task.

Similarity Learning
A type of machine learning where the goal is to learn a function that measures similarity between inputs.

Similarity Measure
A metric used to quantify the similarity between two objects or data points.

Simplex
A geometric object that generalizes the notion of a triangle or tetrahedron to higher dimensions.

Simulated Annealing
A stochastic optimization technique used to find the global minimum of a function by gradually reducing the search space.

Simulation
The process of creating a model of a real-world system or process and experimenting with it to understand how it works.

Sine Wave
A type of wave that oscillates between positive and negative values, with a shape that follows the pattern of the sine function.

Singular Value Decomposition (SVD)
A matrix factorization technique that breaks down a matrix into three separate matrices to find the most important features of the data.

Siri
A virtual assistant developed by Apple Inc. that uses natural language processing to answer questions and perform tasks on behalf of the user.

Sketch-to-Image Synthesis
A type of image generation where a rough sketch is used as input to generate a realistic image.

Skewed Distribution
A distribution where the majority of the data is concentrated on one side of the mean, resulting in a long tail on the other side.

Skewness
A measure of the asymmetry of a probability distribution.

Skill-Based Learning
A type of learning where the focus is on developing specific skills or abilities.

Skymind
A company that develops open-source artificial intelligence software for enterprise use.

SLAM (Simultaneous Localization and Mapping)
A technique used in robotics to build a map of an unknown environment while simultaneously tracking the robot's position within that environment.

Slope
The steepness of a line on a graph.

Small Data
A dataset that is relatively small in size, usually consisting of
a few hundred to a few thousand data points.

SME (Subject Matter Expert)
An individual who has expertise in a specific field or subject
area.

Social Network Analysis
The study of social networks to understand how individuals
are connected and how information or influence spreads
through the network.

Soft Voting
A type of ensemble learning where the predictions of multiple
models are combined using a weighted average.

Softmax
A mathematical function that converts a vector of values into
a probability distribution.

Softmax Regression
A type of logistic regression where the output is a probability
distribution over several discrete outcomes.

SOM (Self-Organizing Map)
A type of artificial neural network used for clustering and
visualization of high-dimensional data.

Spark MLlib
A library of machine learning algorithms

Sparse Autoencoder
A neural network that is used to learn a compressed
representation of data, where the majority of the output
values are zero.

Sparse Coding
A technique used to represent data in a high-dimensional space, where most of the dimensions are zero or close to zero.

Sparse Matrix
A matrix where most of the elements are zero.

Sparse Representation
A representation of data where only a few dimensions are used to represent the data, with most of the other dimensions being zero or close to zero.

Spatial Convolution
A mathematical operation used in deep learning to apply a filter to an image or other spatial data.

Spatial Data
Data that has a spatial component, such as geographic or location data.

Spatial Pyramid Pooling (SPP)
A technique used in computer vision to improve the performance of image classification by dividing an image into regions and pooling the features in each region at different scales.

Spatial Transformation
A transformation applied to spatial data, such as a rotation or translation.

Spatial-temporal data
Data that has both a spatial and a temporal component, such as climate data or traffic data.

Spectral Clustering
A technique used in machine learning to group data points together based on their similarity in a high-dimensional space.

Speech Recognition
AI that enables a computer to recognize and understand human speech.

Spiking Neural Network
A type of neural network that uses the timing of spikes in individual neurons to encode information.

SPSS (Statistical Package for the Social Sciences)
A software package used for statistical analysis in social sciences, such as psychology and sociology.

SQL (Structured Query Language)
A programming language used to manage and manipulate relational databases.

Stacked Autoencoder
A type of neural network that is made up of multiple layers of autoencoders, which are used to learn a compressed representation of data.

Stanford CoreNLP
A suite of natural language processing tools developed by Stanford University that can be used to analyze and parse text.

Star schema
A type of database schema used in data warehousing where a central fact table is surrounded by multiple dimension tables, forming a star-like shape.

State Space Model
A statistical model used to describe a system's behavior over time.

Stationarity
A property of time-series data where the statistical properties of the data do not change over time.

Statistical Learning
A branch of machine learning that focuses on building models that can make predictions based on data.

Stochastic Gradient Descent
An optimization algorithm used in machine learning to minimize the loss function by iteratively adjusting the weights of a model.

Structured Data
Data that is organized in a structured format, such as in a table with columns and rows.

Supervised Learning
A type of machine learning where the algorithm is trained on labeled data, meaning that the data is already classified or labeled.

Support Vector Machine (SVM)
A type of machine learning algorithm that is used for classification and regression analysis. It finds a line or a hyperplane that best separates the different classes of data.

Swarm Intelligence
A type of artificial intelligence that is inspired by the behavior of groups of animals. It uses decentralized decision-making to solve complex problems.

Swift
A programming language that is used to develop applications for iOS, macOS, watchOS, and tvOS. It is designed to be safe, fast, and easy to use.

Symmetric Encryption
A method of encryption where the same key is used for both encrypting and decrypting the data.

Symmetric Multiprocessing (SMP)
A type of computer architecture where multiple processors share the same memory and access to the same data.

Synthetic Data
Artificial data that is generated by a computer program. It is used when real data is not available or when the real data is too sensitive or difficult to obtain.

Synthetic Minority Over-sampling Technique (SMOTE)
A method used in machine learning to balance imbalanced datasets. It creates synthetic data points for the minority class to make it equal to the majority class.

System Identification
A process of building mathematical models of dynamic systems using observed data. It is used to understand how the system behaves and to make predictions about future behavior.

T

T-SNE

A machine learning algorithm used for visualizing high-dimensional data in a two- or three-dimensional space. It is commonly used for data visualization and pattern recognition.

Tacotron

A deep learning model used for text-to-speech synthesis. It converts written text into spoken words using neural networks.

Tensor

A mathematical object used to represent vectors, matrices, and other geometric objects. It is used extensively in machine learning and deep learning.

TensorFlow

A popular open-source software library used for building and training machine learning models. It was developed by Google and is used by many researchers and companies worldwide.

Text Mining

The process of extracting useful information from unstructured text data. It is used to analyze large amounts of text data, such as social media posts, customer reviews, and news articles.

Text recognition

The process of converting handwritten or printed text into digital form. It is used in optical character recognition (OCR) systems to recognize text in scanned documents.

U

U-Net
A convolutional neural network architecture that is commonly used for image segmentation tasks.

Unbalanced Classes
A situation where the classes in a classification problem are not represented equally in the training data.

Uncertainty
A lack of knowledge or information about something that makes it difficult to predict or make decisions about.

Underfitting
A situation where a machine learning model is not complex enough to capture the patterns in the data and performs poorly on both the training and test data.

Uniform Distribution
A probability distribution where each possible outcome is equally likely.

Universal Approximation Theorem
A theorem that states that a neural network with a single hidden layer and a sufficient number of neurons can approximate any continuous function.

Unsupervised Learning
A type of machine learning where the model is trained on unlabeled data and must learn to find patterns and structure on its own.

Up-sampling
The process of increasing the resolution or size of an image
by adding new pixels.

User Experience (UX)
The overall experience that a user has when interacting with
a product or service.

User Interface (UI)
The visual and interactive elements that allow a user to
interact with a product or service.

U-Net
A convolutional neural network architecture that is commonly
used for image segmentation tasks.

Unbalanced Classes
A situation where the classes in a classification problem are
not represented equally in the training data.

V

Validation
The process of evaluating a machine learning model on a separate dataset to assess its performance and generalizeability.

Vanishing Gradient Problem
A problem that can occur during training of deep neural networks where the gradients become very small and the network fails to learn.

Vapnik-Chervonenkis (VC) theory
A theoretical framework for analyzing the generalization ability of machine learning algorithms.

Variance
A statistical measure of how spread out the data is around the mean.

Variational Autoencoder (VAE)
A type of neural network that learns to represent data in a compressed format, and can be used for tasks like image generation and data compression.

Vector Space Model (VSM)
A way of representing text documents as numerical vectors, where each dimension of the vector represents a different word in the document.

VGG
A convolutional neural network architecture that is often used as a benchmark for image recognition tasks.

Video Analytics
The process of analyzing video data using techniques like object detection, tracking, and recognition.

Virtual Assistant
A software program that can perform tasks or provide information for a user through voice or text-based interactions.

Virtual Reality (VR)
A computer-generated simulation of a three-dimensional environment that can be interacted with using special equipment like headsets or gloves.

Vision
The ability to see and interpret visual information. In the context of artificial intelligence, this refers to the ability of computers to analyze and understand visual information.

Visual Recognition
The ability of a computer to identify objects, scenes, and other visual information in images or videos.

Visualization
The process of representing data or information in a visual format like charts, graphs, or maps.

Voice Recognition
The process of converting spoken words into text using speech recognition technology.

W

Watson
A question-answering computer system developed by IBM that uses natural language processing and machine learning algorithms.

Wavenet
A deep neural network architecture used for generating realistic-sounding speech.

Web Scraping
The process of automatically extracting data from websites using software tools.

Weight Decay
A technique used in machine learning to prevent overfitting by adding a penalty term to the loss function based on the size of the model's weights.

Weight Initialization
The process of setting the initial values of a neural network's weights, which can affect the model's ability to learn.

Weight Sharing
A technique used in neural network architectures where the same set of weights is used for multiple parts of the network, allowing it to learn common features more efficiently.

Weighted Average
A type of average where each data point is multiplied by a weight before being added together.

Weighted Decision Tree

A decision tree algorithm where different parts of the tree are assigned different weights, allowing it to make more accurate predictions for certain parts of the data.

Weighted Support Vector Machine (WSVM)

A machine learning algorithm used for classification tasks that assigns weights to different data points to account for class imbalance.

Wide Residual Network (WRN)

A deep neural network architecture that is designed to be more computationally efficient than other deep learning models.

Word Embedding

A way of representing words as numerical vectors, where words that have similar meanings are located close to each other in vector space.

Word2Vec

A popular algorithm for creating word embeddings that uses a neural network to learn word representations based on their context.

Y

YOLO
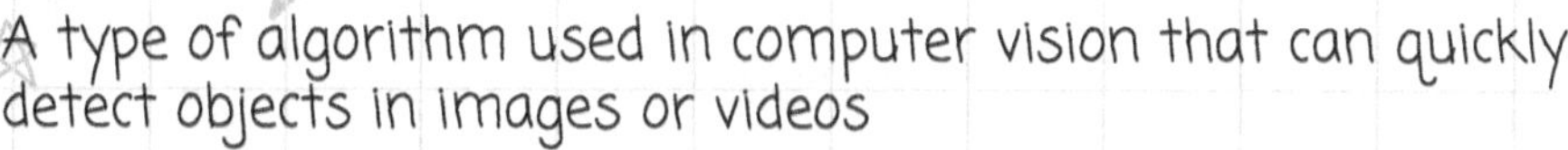
A type of algorithm used in computer vision that can quickly detect objects in images or videos

Z

Z-score
A measure of how many standard deviations a data point is from the mean

Z-test
A statistical test used to determine if there is a significant difference between two sample means

Zero Padding
Adding zeros to the beginning or end of a signal to make it a specific length or size

Zero Shot Learning
A type of machine learning where a model can learn to recognize new categories of objects it hasn't seen before

Zipf's Law
A statistical law that describes the relationship between the frequency of a word in a language and its rank

References

Sources consulted for the encyclopedia:

- BBC Bitesize. (n.d.). What is Artificial Intelligence?
  https://www.bbc.co.uk/bitesize/topics/zgdmsbk/articles/zfkhbdm

- Cognitive Class. (2019). A Beginner's Guide to A.I.
  https://cognitiveclass.ai/courses/ai-for-everyone/

- Future of Life Institute. (2015). Research Priorities for Robust and
  Beneficial Artificial Intelligence.
  https://futureoflife.org/background/research-priorities-ai/

- Wired. (2017). The Ethics of Artificial Intelligence.
  https://www.wired.com/story/the-ethics-of-artificial-intelligence/

- Russell, S. J., & Norvig, P. (2010). Artificial Intelligence: A Modern
  Approach. Prentice Hall.

- ChatGPT, Midjourney A.I and Deepai.org for images and facts.

A. Onkar writes about Artificial Intelligence topics for young adults and kids. Onkar is a versatile technology leader with over 15 years of experience in AI product management, fintech, analytics and engineering, working with various Fortune 100 companies.

Apart from his leadership experience in the corporate and startup world, Onkar is also passionate about academics and has delivered multiple sessions on AI entrepreneurship, machine learning, and analytics at premier business and engineering schools.

Onkar believes A.I. literacy is globally indispensable for the present generation, but true access to A.I. is still confined to the high priests in Silicon Valley. With engaging articles, interactive activities, and real-world examples of AI in action, Onkar hopes to democratize access to A.I. and inspire a new generation of young readers to explore the exciting world of technology that matters as they grow up.

With this vision, Onkar has authored "A.I. Encyclopedia for Kids : Artificial Intelligence for All" - The jargon-free, concise, storyboarded articles explain the basic concepts of AI in a way that's easy for beginners and kids to understand.